Accession no.
00925145

Department ... ...ce

WITHDRAWN

LIBRARY

Tel: 01244 375444   Ext: 3301

This book is to be returned on or before the
last date stamped below. Overdue charges
will be incurred by the late return of books.

Chester

A College of the
University of Liverpool

KT-567-629

UCC LIBRARY
14 DEC 2001

27 FEB 2004   CANCELLED

30 JUL 2004

UCC LIBRARY
21 DEC 2001

06 AUG 2004

NOV 2006   CANCELLED

CANCELLED

18 APR 2006   CANCELLED

UCC LIBRARY
23 APR 2002

CANCELLED

-7 DEC 2003

CANCELLED

Week
Loan

© Crown Copyright 1989
First published 1989
Second impression 1990

ISBN 0 11 270684 3

Printed in the United Kingdom for HMSO.
Dd 292403 3/90 C50

Contents

CHESTER COLLEGE

ACC No.
00925145

DEPT.
OWL

CLASS No.
375.6137 EDU

LIBRARY

Preface

Since 1984 HM Inspectorate has published a number of Curriculum Matters papers designed to stimulate discussion about the curriculum as a whole and its component parts.

Physical education from 5 to 16, the sixteenth in the series, sets out a framework within which schools might develop a programme for the teaching and learning of physical education appropriate to their pupils.

Like other earlier publications in the Curriculum Matters series, it is a discussion paper intended to stimulate professional debate and to contribute to reaching national agreement about the objectives and content of the school curriculum. That debate will now take place within the arrangements for developing the National Curriculum contained in the Education Reform Act, particularly through the work of the National Curriculum Council (NCC). Physical education is one of the foundation subjects of the National Curriculum which will be required to be taught to all pupils of compulsory school age in maintained schools. It is hoped that this paper will contribute to the continuing debate about the nature of physical education in our schools.

This document should be read as a whole, since all sections are interrelated.

Introduction

1. For many people physical education is synonymous with physical recreation, playing games, keeping fit or taking part in a variety of physical pursuits. Team games, athletics, tennis, gymnastics, dance, swimming, outdoor pursuits and a range of other activities are each undertaken by large numbers of people in their leisure time. In the school curriculum, however, these activities take place in a context of teaching and learning. In physical education general and specific skills are acquired, knowledge and understanding developed, and positive attitudes and personal and social attributes encouraged.

The aims of physical education

2. Physical education in schools aims to contribute to the development of control, co-ordination and mastery of the body. It is primarily concerned with a way of learning through action, sensation and observation. It is possible to gain knowledge of physical activities in a theoretical way but skills can be acquired only by personal experience of movement. Such experience, which requires thought as well as effort, leads to improved performance, personal achievement, understanding and increased knowledge. Satisfaction and enjoyment arise from working with a sense of purpose and practising hard enough and long enough to overcome the challenges presented by the practical work.

3. The aims of physical education are to:

- develop a range of psycho-motor skills

- maintain and increase physical mobility and flexibility

- develop stamina and strength

- develop understanding and appreciation of the purposes, forms and conventions of a selection of physical activities

- develop the capacity to express ideas in dance forms

- develop the appreciation of the concepts of fair play, honest competition and good sportsmanship

- develop the ability to appreciate the aesthetic qualities of movement

1

- develop the capacity to maintain interest and to persevere to achieve success

- foster self-esteem through the acquisition of physical competence and poise

- develop self-confidence through understanding the capabilities and limitations of oneself and others

- develop an understanding of the importance of exercise in maintaining a healthy life.

Curricular objectives

4. Within these broad aims there are more precise goals or objectives towards which pupils work. Because of children's individual differences and talents, they achieve certain objectives at different times and with different degrees of competence. Defining objectives clearly brings a sense of order to the work so that learning is broadly progressive and later learning builds on earlier experiences. Interpreted flexibly, objectives allow opportunities for extending children's experiences along the avenues which open up during the course of the work. Without such flexibility there would be a loss of the essential element of spontaneity in teaching and learning. The following objectives indicate a range of expectations for children of different ages, though the extent to which some can be developed will be dependent upon the availability of facilities, time and support. They offer the basic guidelines to facilitate continuity and progression in learning.

Objectives for 7-year-old pupils

5. Learning by doing and moving is crucial to the physical, intellectual, emotional and social education of young children. On entry to school some show greater physical competence than others, but all need frequent and regular opportunities for physical activity in order to develop, to learn by doing and feeling and to satisfy their need to be active. For young children many actions regarded as simple or taken for granted by older people represent a considerable challenge, for example, to hop, to skip, to jump, to catch an object. Achieving a degree of control in such actions brings children real delight which leads them to repeat the actions over and over again. Work for this age group needs to be planned to allow plenty of time for practice

2

and repetition with help given to make children think about their actions and become increasingly aware of what they are able to do. Equally they need variety, not only because their span of concentration is limited but also so that their range and scope of movement are extended in interesting situations.

6. By the age of 7 children should have had experiences which enable them to:

- perform confidently, though with varying degrees of control and co-ordination, basic ways of moving from one place to another, for example, running, jumping, rolling, climbing, transferring weight from one part of the body to another and holding the body still

- appreciate and use contrast in speed, in effort and in spatial aspects, for example, quick/slow, strong/light, wide/narrow, high/low

- use apparatus to get on/off, under/over, along

- absorb shock when jumping or moving from apparatus of various heights

- appreciate, and respond to, contrasting sounds in music, percussion and words and to be able to react to simple rhythms

- convey through movement the elements contained in a story and to express appropriate characteristics and moods

- propel a variety of objects, for example, balls of appropriate sizes, quoits, hoops

- catch or receive objects providing these are sent in such a way as to require simple judgements of speed and trajectory and little adjustment of the body or its position

- play simple games with, and alongside, others and with simple rules of their own and the teacher's devising, thereby experiencing membership of a team

- be confident in water and able to move themselves through water with or without buoyancy aids

- share and take care of apparatus and equipment

- lift, carry and place apparatus carefully.

Objectives for 11-year-old pupils

7. From 7 to 11 years, children's motor skills, control and co-ordination develop greatly and the programme of work in physical education should help extend and refine these. Within the tasks set, children are often spontaneous and inventive and these qualities should be encouraged. Work also needs to be planned to provide the children with opportunities for practice, repetition and imitation so that their earlier learning is consolidated and skill enhanced. Increasing knowledge and experience gradually extend children's ability to tackle new and more complex tasks. At the same time they increasingly enjoy and learn through working in co-operation with others, and through competition with their peers.

8. By the age of 11 children should have had experiences which enable them to:

- combine basic actions such as ways of travelling and turning to produce sequences showing a degree of continuity with appropriate variation of speed and effort

- perform sequences on the floor and on apparatus of different heights, for example, bench, wall-bars, ropes, trestles and platforms

- repeat and refine their own sequences

- copy sequences devised by others

- reproduce some specific movement patterns, for example, in named skills such as handstands

- select actions appropriate to the task and to the apparatus

- absorb shock and momentum and receive their weight appropriately according to the preceding action

- respond physically to rhythms, moods, qualities in music, words and sounds

- develop and repeat phrases of movement in dance

- express simple ideas and feelings clearly using a range of gestures and actions

- strike or propel a ball with reasonable accuracy by using different parts of the body and a variety of implements

- anticipate cause and effect, for example, flight of a ball, movement of others

- invent their own games, selecting appropriate equipment, size and shape of playing area and numbers of participants

- participate in team games involving variable numbers of players

- conform to rules including those of their own devising

- swim on front and back and be confident in water

- enter water safely by jumping or using an elementary dive

- perform certain skills in water, for example, tread water and float

- carry and use a range of apparatus responsibly and carefully.

Objectives for 16-year-old pupils

9.   During the secondary phase of schooling pupils' physical, intellectual and emotional development proceeds at widely differing rates. The effects are seen in such factors as increased height, weight, strength and endurance. At the same time, there may be marked changes in social and emotional behaviour. While many pupils maintain steady progress towards greater motor control and co-ordination, some at the age of 16 are still growing and may experience a marked unevenness in skill levels in these circumstances. Their increased understanding may be demonstrated not in physical performance but in more mature attitudes and enhanced appreciation of good movement. Between 11 and 16 it is important for all pupils to continue with regular physical activity which places increasing demands on them, improves flexibility and mobility, builds up strength and stamina and develops self-confidence so that they willingly participate in worthwhile activities at school and in leisure pursuits in later life.

10.   By the age of 16 pupils should have had experiences which enable them with varying degrees of skill to:

- invent and improvise sequences in gymnastics and dance relating to the objectives set by themselves or others or in response to a variety of stimuli

5

- perform and be able to replicate sequences with precision, showing continuity and flow in movement
- choreograph dances
- use and adapt skills in sequence or combination taking into account changing circumstances
- participate in a variety of games including large and small team games and individual sports
- know the principles of attack and defence in relation to several games
- take different roles in several games
- devise practices and tactics for specific purposes
- know and observe the rules of games in which they participate
- act as officials
- swim using a variety of strokes
- use personal survival skills in water
- understand and use life-saving skills
- know the effect of different kinds of intensities of physical exercise on the body
- develop an understanding of stress, relaxation, fatigue, rest and endurance
- appraise the performance of themselves and others
- respond sensitively to the expressive qualities of movement.

11.   In addition to pursuing the objectives specific to physical education pupils should acquire other more general skills and positive attitudes. They should, for example, develop their powers of observation. Young children can only observe effectively one performer at a time showing short, relatively simple movements; they need to have their attention suitably directed and to be asked simple questions about what they have seen. Older pupils, with practice, can observe more than one performer demonstrating various actions and can express ideas about why the performance is good and how it can be improved.

Children are usually generous and warm-hearted in their responses and such consideration and respect for others need to be fostered. At the same time the ability to criticise constructively and to be able to accept criticism should also be developed. By the time they leave school, pupils should be able to deal with quite complex situations requiring keen observation, to make independent use of their observation to improve their own performance and to apply their knowledge to express critical appreciation.

12. Similarly the ability to listen to instructions, translate them into action and to visualise the circumstances as they affect people, space and apparatus and safety can be developed progressively. From the initial stages of reacting to short, simple instructions through situations in which instructions gradually become more complicated, pupils should ultimately be able to interpret an idea which requires them to devise and organise their own tasks, to choose their own apparatus, accompaniment or stimulus and to be able to explain their intentions clearly to others. In the same way they can be encouraged to remember and reproduce work of gradually increasing complexity, through rehearsing actions both mentally and physically.

13. Physical skills are not always easily acquired and require a degree of persistence and determination to master them. If tasks are suitably challenging and if there is appropriate help and recognition of progress made, pupils can be encouraged to develop positive attitudes. Similarly, well-structured work which gives pupils explicit opportunities to share ideas and to lead and organise groups, as well as to act independently, can contribute to their personal and social development.

A framework for planning work in physical education

14. The planned nature of the experience in physical education distinguishes it from free play or recreation. Through the careful selection of content, opportunities can be provided to enable skills, knowledge and attitudes to be acquired. A programme of work should be designed to reflect a balance both in the kind of activity and in the processes involved in becoming more skilful, more efficient and more fluent within that

7

activity. A balance is also necessary between breadth and depth of content. Other factors, too, such as continuity, frequency and intensity must be considered if the work is to be satisfying and progressive.

15. Not all aspects of physical education require the same amount of time or the same degree of continuity for progress to be made. Some activities, because of their complexity, need to be practised regularly. Gymnastics is one example where considerable time is needed to develop bodily skills and agility, the ability to produce sequences and the confidence to apply these to the use of apparatus. Some flexibility in planning the length and timing of courses for the various elements can help to develop a programme which is both varied and demanding.

16. For older pupils it may be valuable and appropriate, if facilities allow, to give opportunities for choice which take account of pupils' different interests and capabilities. However, care needs to be taken to ensure that all pupils continue to pursue a balanced and worthwhile programme. It is important to consider pupils' immediate needs as well as introducing them to a range of activities which they are likely to be involved in as young adults.

17. One framework for planning a balanced programme in physical education identifies five different aspects:

● the development of skilful body management

● creative and aesthetic experience through movement

● competitive activities among groups and individuals

● body training leading to increased strength and stamina and endurance

● challenging experiences in a variety of outdoor environments.

Such an approach to planning implies that the content of a balanced curriculum is not simply a series of particular activities but rather the medium through which all the essential aspects of physical education are experienced. Individual activities are selected according to the particular contribution they make to one or more of the aspects of physical education. Account needs to be taken of the ways in which some activities complement and reinforce each other.

18. Although the framework outlined above is particularly applicable to the secondary phase it needs to be suitably interpreted to inform work with younger children. In primary schools the body training element is less important than others. Stamina and strength can be developed at this stage through opportunities for frequent vigorous activity. Swimming-pools and apparatus in gymnastics provide challenging settings for activity and the range can be extended by including activities such as camping, walking and other outdoor pursuits. For primary pupils the first three aspects in the framework are of prime significance and can be well served by the gymnastics, dance, games, swimming and athletics most commonly provided as part of the primary curriculum.

19. **Gymnastics** is concerned with acquiring control, co-ordination and versatility in the use of the body. It is based on natural actions such as jumping, leaping, balancing, rolling, pushing, pulling and swinging. At the primary stage these natural actions need to be explored and refined so that the variety of each can be experienced, practised and consolidated, leading to improvement in performance and application in new contexts. The actions also need to be combined so that children learn how to blend movements appropriately.

20. At secondary level, gymnastics work becomes more precise, subtle and complex in its forms. With varying degrees of skill pupils should be able to work on the floor and on apparatus to compose sequences of movement, which show appropriate dynamic qualities, fluency and control. They should also be able to perform some specific gymnastic skills. These, however, need to be carefully taught and closely matched to individual levels of competence. Pupils of this age also enjoy working with partners or in small groups if they are sufficiently mature to cope with problems of timing, and to take responsibility for the safety of others and the sharing of ideas. The range of apparatus usually available in secondary schools can increase the challenge either in terms of height, surface or distance or by pieces used in combination. The response of pupils can, therefore, be extended whether they work individually or in groups.

21. Lessons in gymnastics should, whenever possible, include opportunities to work at floor level and on apparatus. Apparatus helps to develop pupils' experience by requiring them to work on, or over, varied surfaces at different heights and to

9

judge height, width, length and distance. It also increases the possibilities of movement by giving opportunities to swing, circle or climb, to support the body in different ways and to allow movement below the level of the supporting part or surface. Perhaps even more significantly, the use of apparatus involves the application and extension of ideas established in floor work, the solving of practical problems and the making of decisions about what actions are appropriate and where these can be performed.

22. **Dance**, too, focusses on developing mastery of the body. Like gymnastics it helps maintain flexibility and mobility and develops an appreciation of line, form, strength and grace in movement. Much of its content is closely allied to that in gymnastics and may be explored in similar ways, though the purposes of dance will be better served by using movement which communicates and evokes emotion. In dance, gesture, phrasing, rhythm and awareness of the use of space in the patterns made by the body are of greater significance than in gymnastics. Most importantly the intention in dance is to use the body expressively, often to convey ideas or moods. Pupils, therefore, need to be made increasingly aware of the manner or style of their movement, for example, moving lightly, suddenly, smoothly, and becoming more able to control its qualitative effect.

23. During the primary school years, the emphasis should be on the experience of dancing and making dances which are not closely structured and are unlikely to be recalled or repeated in exactly the same way. Much of children's experience should consist of responding spontaneously to stimuli which have been carefully chosen for their evocative qualities, for example, records, poetry, percussion instruments. Ideas used to stimulate movement or dramatic response can often stem from aspects of classwork or arise from natural happenings, such as a fall of snow or a windy day. Children should also be helped to become aware of phrases or patterns of movement, to consider how these begin and end, and to repeat or reproduce them, thereby creating their own rhythms.

24. At the secondary stage, opportunities should be provided for dancing which includes social dances of different cultures and periods, for making dances and for developing knowledge and appreciation of dance and dancers. The range of stimuli

may be similar to those used at earlier stages but the ideas presented need to match the increasing sophistication of the pupils. For example, a fairground may be an appropriate starting-point for younger pupils but older groups might deal with more abstract ideas such as friendship and loneliness. Music used should be drawn from a wide variety of styles and periods and increasingly allow pupils to use rhythms in a subtle and imaginative way rather than be dominated by them. Technical skill and understanding will need to be developed if pupils are to be able to express themselves with greater clarity and precision and to work with increasing sensitivity with other dancers. The craft of composition can be developed by creating individual, small group and large group dances and can contribute towards an appreciation of the demands of performance in terms of presentation. Appreciation of dance, both as audience and performer, can be fostered through experience, knowledge and the opportunity to reflect on what has been seen or done and to talk about it using technical and non-technical language. In this way dance can make an important contribution to the aesthetic and creative area of learning and experience.

25. The main features of **games** are the development of motor skills, hand and eye co-ordination, tactics and strategies and the matching of this range of skills against an opponent or other challenge within a framework of rules. Games take many forms but, in the context of physical education, they produce a high degree of physical activity, physical skills, mental alertness and reaction.

26. Games invariably involve competition. From an early stage children compete, first against themselves ('how many times can I — ?', 'how far can I — ?') and then against a friend ('who can catch the most times?', 'who can hit a target?') and then with a friend against others. However, concentration on this element can distract pupils from thinking about the skills being practised and so can impede learning. The major emphasis for young children should be on sharing and working together. But the fun of simple competition undertaken in good humour and within a framework of simple rules should not be denied to them. As they get older, children become increasingly interested in adult forms of recognised games and wish to play 'the proper game'. In games lessons, whether pupils are competing one against one, in small or large groups or teams,

11

the emphasis should be on the application of practised physical skills and on the development of the skills of team play. Most pupils wish to be in a team and play in a match and opportunities can be provided, without unbalancing the work undertaken, to answer this need for all. More able pupils, whatever their chosen game or activity, continue to want to extend their skill and pit their wits against opponents of similar ability. This interest can and should be fostered both in and outside school. But in timetabled time, lessons must be planned to satisfy the needs of all pupils and the range of extra-curricular activities provided should accommodate a broad range of ability and interests. Any game with a team, however small, is about co-operation as well as competition; both elements need to be stressed so that the manner of taking part depends upon skill, teamwork and the acceptance of rules.

27. In primary schools, games lessons should give pupils opportunities to run, chase, dodge and change direction so that they become agile, alert and controlled in their use of space. Pupils should use balls and bats of different shapes, sizes and weights so that they develop the ability to throw, bounce, catch, strike, kick and travel with a ball. They should work individually or with partners, often in games which they invent. Such activities help children to adapt to moving objects, to move and prepare the body appropriately for action and to use space effectively. These skills are not easily acquired because many elements are involved. Pupils require much regular practice in situations which gradually increase in difficulty. Inventing games involves children in working co-operatively to agree some or all the circumstances in which their play takes place, for example how the game is started and re-started, how points or goals are scored, the composition of teams, the equipment to be used, the shape and extent of the playing area. When they have developed and refined a game, children can show it to others, explain it and help others to play. Early or undue emphasis on recognised games, which are often complex, should be avoided. The games children play at this stage should have teams and playing areas which are small enough to ensure maximum involvement and to keep the problems associated with 'reading' the game at a level with which they can cope and experience success and satisfaction.

28. At the secondary stage, there is a large range of formal games which pupils might experience. However, given the con-

straints of time, facilities, staffing and numbers of pupils, decisions have to be made about how a balance between depth and type of experience is to be achieved in this aspect of work and within the context of the total curriculum in physical education. Games may be categorised in a number of ways, for example net games (tennis, badminton, volleyball), striking/ fielding games (rounders, cricket), invasion games (rugby and association football, lacrosse, basketball, netball, hockey) and wall/court games (squash, fives). The categories identify the characteristics of different types of games. Applying a system of categorisation of games to select the components of pupils' experience can help in achieving balance in the provision and in identifying where activities are complementary and where reinforcement can occur.

29. By the time pupils reach the secondary school, skill levels have increased (and continue to increase) and interest in formal games has developed. Much of the work in games lessons will be focussed on the development of specific skills and tactical awareness. Though important, the acquisition of skills needs to be seen in the context of developing understanding and knowledge of principles. Skills should be related to and applied in the game so that players see their purpose and place. Adaptation in size of team or area, equipment and rules can be made to assist learning. Opportunities to invent games continue to help pupils to apply skills and appreciate the principles of play. Throughout, pupils need to be encouraged to take some responsibility for their own learning and to be able to work with, and help, others.

30. **Swimming** and **athletics** generally have a place within the physical education curriculum though the extent to which they can be developed is affected by the availability of facilities on or off the school site. It is beneficial if the opportunity to learn to **swim** can be given as early as possible during the primary phase, when the emphasis needs to be on developing safety and confidence in the water, and the acquisition of the fundamentals of certain recognised strokes: a child who learns to swim at the primary stage is more likely to become a proficient swimmer subsequently. At the secondary level, attention should be on improving technique and increasing the number of strokes used as well as on survival and life-saving skills and, when circumstances allow, diving and synchronised swimming.

31. **Athletics** in the primary school seeks to develop children's natural capacities to run, jump and throw without undue emphasis on competition or on the recognised formal events of athletics. These events can be more fully explored and experienced in the secondary school when the mechanical principles can be better understood and applied. Some pupils will develop ability and interest in particular track or field events, but for others, the knowledge and experience of mechanical principles, physiological effects, the preparation of the body for activity and appreciation of training schedules can be of value in promoting a positive attitude towards care and respect for the body. This can be translated into the practice of an active and healthy life-style after pupils leave school.

32. The provision of **outdoor pursuits** is dependent upon the accessibility of facilities and expertise among the staff. However, much can be done at school or in the immediate area, for example, by pitching a tent or cooking a simple meal. For safety reasons, activities such as sailing, canoeing and climbing make heavy demands on staffing resources as one adult can be responsible for only a small number of pupils. Where provision is difficult within curriculum time, many schools try to give such experiences through extra-curricular clubs and weekend expeditions and as an aspect of residential experience.

The cross-curricular aspects of physical education

33. In primary schools, the physical education of pupils is usually the responsibility of the class teacher. This arrangement provides opportunities for links to be made relatively easily between physical education and other areas of work, not only in the aims and content but also in the way children learn and apply their knowledge and skills. For example, through experience in physical education children can be helped to understand mathematical and linguistic concepts such as large and small, heavy and light, wide and narrow, symmetry and asymmetry. They can also learn to understand spatial relationships as they move forwards, backwards, sideways and diagonally; to estimate size and distance and to comprehend the ideas of above and below, between and through. The development of language can be encouraged as the meaning of words is illustrated in

action. Children's abilities to talk about what they do and see, to describe using technical and non-technical language, to express ideas, to organise and to give instructions should all be fostered in physical education lessons.

34. Specialist teachers of physical education in secondary schools need to relate work in the subject with that in other areas. The importance of diet and the care of the body are concerns of health education, home economics and physical education. Practical work in physical education can extend and apply the information and knowledge about health acquired in other lessons. The practical experience and application of principles and laws concerning action and reaction, levers, momentum, floating and sinking can reinforce pupils' learning in science. Both dance and drama are collaborative arts in which ideas are shared in improvisation, in which feelings and relationships are explored and in which responses are gradually shaped to achieve clarity of intention and presentation. The experience of different forms of expression and communication can enhance the work undertaken in both subjects. Physical education produces many opportunities to contribute to pupils' personal, social and moral development; for example in the sharing and showing of work; in co-operative activities including the experience of leading and following; in appreciating and accepting the different abilities and qualities of their peers; in the concept of fair play and the observance of rules. To exploit the possibilities, these aspects need to be made explicit and discussed with pupils.

35. A well-balanced physical education programme should meet the physical and social needs of all pupils in an ethnically diverse society. Physical education should ensure that all pupils have an opportunity to participate on equal terms in a range of activities and should help them to develop their self-esteem through achievement. The shared nature of the activities provides opportunities for pupils to appreciate the achievements, ideas and efforts of others, to understand similarities and differences, and, on occasion, to work together towards a common goal. In some activities such as dance where the focus is on the exploration of feelings and attitudes, there is considerable scope for the recognition and understanding of common human qualities. The different experiences which children bring with them from their diverse backgrounds, such as formal and informal games or styles and traditions of dance

can be exploited to broaden appreciation of the cultural variety in society. However, particularly as boys and girls mature, sensitivity is required to issues related to the varied backgrounds of pupils, for example over changing arrangements and the wearing of suitable clothing. Some modifications in the programme may also be necessary to ensure that there are opportunities for single-sex activities taught by a teacher of the same sex. For pupils for whom English is a second language care needs to be taken over the way in which tasks are presented and explanations given. The language used should be non-technical, appropriate and relevant to the pupils, and should help to broaden their vocabulary.

36.   Physical activities make a significant contribution to the extra-curricular programmes of schools. Such activities should be planned so as to extend the experiences offered in the physical education curriculum for as many pupils of all abilities as possible. Pupils may pursue interests in club activities; some might assist in the running of clubs or organise them themselves; physically able pupils can develop skill and understanding to a high level by taking part in competitive experiences and team practices; new activities can be introduced which might otherwise not be possible within the constraints of curriculum time, facilities and staffing.

37.   As pupils approach the end of the compulsory years of schooling, it is important that they appreciate the wide range of sporting and recreational activities available, many of which cannot be experienced at school because of the constraints of time, costs and resources. They should be informed about and, where possible, put in contact with the providers of sport and recreation in the wider community such as local clubs and sports centres. They should also know how and where they can obtain information or gain access to further training through such agencies as governing bodies of sport, local and regional sports councils, local authority recreation departments, colleges of further education, youth organisations and adult education.

Principles of teaching and learning

38.   Since pupils develop and learn at different rates and in different ways the aims and objectives of physical education should be pursued through a variety of teaching and learning

styles. There needs to be a finely adjusted balance between different approaches to learning and instruction dependent in part on the objectives of particular lessons. At one time, a highly analytical procedure demanding close and detailed observation of movement and repeated practice with correction, guidance and attention to technical detail may be required. At another, the introduction of an element of spontaneity and play-like activity may result in delight in movements performed without conscious analysis.

39. At times it will be necessary to teach common points to the class: these will be based on the teacher's observation and knowledge and also upon suggestions which pupils themselves contribute and upon the provision of common experience deliberately planned by the teacher. At other times, teaching will be conducted on an individual or small group basis, again drawing upon pupils' ideas when possible and appropriate. While it is often necessary to practise constituent parts of a movement or action, it can be helpful to get the feel of the whole movement at the outset. This can be achieved by observing a good performance and then trying to imitate it: for example, in swimming, watching a stroke and then copying rather than practising separate arm and leg actions, though this may be necessary at some stage.

40. Demonstration of movement can be used to serve a variety of purposes. In the example quoted above the purpose is to provide a good model. Demonstrations might also be used to show a variety of ideas and responses to an open-ended task, to illustrate particular teaching points such as the turn of the body and the transference of weight in a throwing action, or to demonstrate the flow of actions in a sequence. Teachers need to be sensitive in their selection of pupils to demonstrate, ensuring that, as far as possible, pupils of different levels of physical ability are given the opportunity to contribute in this way. Young children often enjoy showing their work to others but older pupils may be more self-conscious and prefer to be involved in group rather than individual demonstration. The use of demonstrations by the teacher needs to be handled with the same discrimination. It is usually only necessary when a good model cannot be provided by a pupil. Many teachers, especially primary teachers, often find that 'sketching' part of a movement, using gesture supported by appropriately descriptive words, is sufficient to help pupils gain an impression of what is

17

involved. One of the most important purposes of demonstration is to promote observation, so that pupils can make use of what they see in their own work and also become more perceptive in the appreciation of the performance of others.

41. Rather than always receiving information from the teacher, children can be encouraged to suggest ways in which they think their own work can be improved. This can be extended to helping a partner and to sharing ideas in a group. They can also be given responsibility for their own learning in other ways, for example, by devising tactics in a game, setting up their own practices to improve skills, choosing and arranging apparatus in gymnastics, or constructing a personal programme of exercises for promoting fitness.

42. Physical education is most usually taught in classes which contain pupils who have a wide range of physical competence. Sometimes they may include pupils who are physically gifted and, on occasion, some who have specific physical, mental or sensory disabilities. For the latter, tasks need to be carefully graded and modified but appropriately challenging; individualised schedules need to be prepared, drawing upon the advice and support of teachers and others who have close knowledge of the pupils and their particular problems. For the less able pupils, tasks need to be broken down into simple stages to aid learning and to foster the feeling of success. For the gifted, tasks should be designed to challenge them to think about how to combine, apply and modify their skills and style with versatility and precision. Occasionally, groups may be formed to allow some of the work to be covered at different pace and levels. However, in the main such organisation is not possible. Within a lesson there are many opportunities to present differentiated work in such a way that expectations can be matched to the abilities of the pupils. To make such provision is no easy task. It involves careful planning based on an understanding of pupils' needs, good organisational skills and control, the ability to observe and react appropriately to the differing responses which arise, and the capacity to recall and reflect upon situations to influence subsequent work.

43. Where open-ended tasks requiring individual responses are set, pupils may work to their own capacity and within their own limitations. The teacher, from knowledge of both the material and pupils, has the responsibility of giving individual

or group guidance to improve the work so that each pupil gains satisfaction and enjoyment. Such open-ended tasks, for example in gymnastics, may lead to the need to develop specific skills and abilities. The teacher may judge the appropriate time to intervene to further this development either for individuals or for all the pupils. Frequently class practices of specific skills are introduced too early and this may inhibit spontaneity and versatility or outface those who are not ready or able to cope with the physical demands. It is also important, in these cases, to relate the specific activity back to the more general situation so that its application to the ideas being explored may be understood. For example, a handstand may be selected for practice following a task involving supporting and holding weight on different parts of the body. Following practice of the specific skill, pupils need to return to improving other responses to consolidate the principles of getting the weight of the body directly over appropriately placed points of support.

44. In physical education there are always possibilities for organising learning in a variety of ways – individual, group or whole class. Differentiation in the work can be achieved by the groupings made within the class. Given the opportunity, young children often pair or group themselves according to friendship links though later it is often found that similar abilities influence this choice. The teacher may wish to organise other forms of grouping to allow different targets to be set commensurate with the capacities of the various groups. For example, in games some could practise skills in demanding situations, perhaps of their own choosing, whilst others could work in small numbers, at a slower pace or with fewer skills being combined. In gymnastics, apparatus could be graded in difficulty for groups with different levels of skills and confidence. Activities such as swimming, athletics and fitness work lend themselves to the development of individual schedules of work. Sometimes physically able pupils can be given the responsibility for helping those less able than themselves; equally, pupils who are inventive can be asked to work with others physically more adept but less imaginative.

45. Teachers need to decide whether a reasonable variety and balance of approaches are being provided both within the span of a lesson and in the longer-term programme. They should decide whether the main emphasis should be on the development of work already started or on new work, whether

19

individual exploration or more closely directed practice is appropriate, whether a group organisation would help, and what the balance should be between group or class and individual activities.

Assessment

46. Assessment serves a number of functions. It supplies important information to the teacher; it gives an indication of the level of learning and the proportion of pupils who are finding the work too easy or too difficult and who therefore need to be directed towards more appropriately challenging activities. It can also indicate a poor class response caused by inappropriate organisation or poor development of resources. Assessment can also help with the diagnosis of learning difficulties and point to ways of overcoming them. The pupils themselves can be helped and motivated by the feedback which assessment gives provided they understand the purpose and structure of the tasks in which they are engaged. The contribution of assessment to motivation is particularly relevant for younger children or where the task is complex.

47. A very significant feature of assessment in physical education is that the performance of a sequence of movements, an action or a skill normally leaves no trace: there is nothing permanent to check. Some actions have identifiable results such as the ability to swim a certain distance, which can be recorded, though nothing is necessarily known about the manner and style of their achievement. Pupils can talk and write about physical activities but such understanding and appreciation may not be reflected in their practical attainments. Video recordings of practical work can be helpful in providing material for the teacher and the performer to look at and assess. The process, however, is time-consuming and the use of video recordings must inevitably be a rare event.

48. The main form of assessment must be the continuous process of observation by the teacher based on knowledge of the pupils and of the content of the work. Clarifying objectives and making explicit the criteria which assist the recognition of good performance can help guide observation and provide a consistent base for subjective assessment supplemented, where appropriate, by objective measurement of performance.

Observation should be an unobtrusive part of the teacher's skills and is most effective when it is used in the course of normal teaching. If both subjective and objective assessments are employed over a period of time, a comprehensive picture of the programme of work can be built up which assesses what objectives are being accomplished and how they are being tackled.

49.   Although there is general agreement about what constitutes skilfulness in particular activities, many skills can be performed with varying degrees of success while deviating from the ideal. For example, many children may be able to swim 30 metres using the breast stroke without being able to co-ordinate their legs and arms correctly. If the distance is the objective set it can be an appropriate measure of competence as it stands. The ultimate purpose of teaching, however, is to help children to swim, jump, throw and control the body with increasing skilfulness and to this end teachers need to assess *how* the actions are performed. Compared with the assessment of the outcome of actions, such as distance jumped or thrown, these judgements are not easy to make and need to be informed by knowledge and experience. There is no short cut to acquiring this knowledge: it is obtained by observing examples of good performance, reading, attendance at courses, and continually observing and commenting upon pupils' responses in lessons. The process of observation leading to judgement requires a great deal of practice and is best developed by the teacher concentrating on one or two features of the action. In observing actions the following may assist teachers in clarifying judgements:

Body: the stance/shape/orientation adopted in readiness or in anticipation should be appropriate and body parts should be used effectively with regard to their contribution to the action as should the shape(s) through which the body moves

Space: the successful performer shows a positional sense in relation to objects and people, and to the space available

Dynamics: the muscular tension in the body as a whole and in particular parts should match the nature and intention of the movement and its successful performance. The relative speed of different parts of the body, and of the whole body, should combine to make the movement effective.

21

Other factors to be looked for, particularly as physical competence increases, are consistency, the ability to repeat skilful actions in varying circumstances, adaptability, and the ability to modify skills and deploy them imaginatively in response to different circumstances.

50. When tasks are open-ended and dependent on individual interpretations, assessment becomes more complex but the features already mentioned are still applicable. Consideration also has to be given to the suitability and variety of the actions chosen to answer the task, to the imaginative way in which they have been linked together, and to the dynamic and spatial aspects of movement, particularly as these relate to apparatus, rhythmic accompaniment, partners or groups. In dance, the form and line in action and the relationships with other dancers are important. Sensitivity, the focussing of attention, and the ability to convey through gesture and expression ideas, moods or feelings are also significant. Assessment needs to take account of the experience as a whole, not merely the sum of its parts.

51. In order to chart progress in the acquisition of skills and knowledge and the development of positive attitudes, a longitudinal record of the achievements and responses of pupils is required. This needs to make use of the teacher's routine observations in a quick and easy way combined with occasional comment and also with some assessment from pupils on how they think they are progressing. Such a record can only be achieved if objectives have been defined and criteria established on which to base assessment.

Conclusion

52. Physical education in schools needs to build on children's enjoyment of, and need for, activity and movement. It seeks to develop co-ordination, strength, stamina and skilfulness, and to promote spatial awareness, intelligent reactions to situations and appreciation of physical excellence. It should lead to a sense of well-being, a healthy life-style and a feeling of self-confidence. To achieve these ends it is necessary to establish clear aims and objectives and the means of evaluating their implementation. It is hoped that this paper will contribute to the design of an effective curriculum in physical education.